D0016173

The Countess of Stanlein Restored

V

The Countess of Stanlein Restored

◆

NICHOLAS DELBANCO

VERSO

London • New York

FIRST PUBLISHED BY VERSO 2001

VERSO

UK: 6 MEARD STREET, LONDON W1V OEG
USA: 180 VARICK STREET, NEW YORK, NY 10014-4606

VERSO is an imprint of NEW LEFT BOOKS

Design by POLLEN/Stewart Cauley, Eric Skillman

ISBN 1 85984 761 7

British Library Cataloguing in Publication Data
A catalogue record for this book is available from the British Library

Library of Congress Cataloging-in-Publication Data
A catalog record for this book is available from the Library of Congress

The Countess of Stanlein
ex-Paganini Stradivarius violoncello of 1707.

IT'S 2:30 IN THE MORNING OF THURSDAY, JUNE 1, 2000, and three cellists are fondling a scroll. The cello beneath it stands mute. "Sensuous," says Yo-Yo Ma; "Sensational," says Ko Iwasaki, and Bernard Greenhouse, its owner, traces the instrument's neck. What they examine and praise is one of the world's great wooden stringed resonating boxes: the Countess of Stanlein ex-Paganini Stradivarius violoncello of 1707. "Sensuous," says Ma again, and smiles and shuts his eyes.

This has been a long day. The week-long World Cello Congress III is taking place in Baltimore, and more than five hundred musicians flock to master classes and panels and recitals both exhaustive and exhausting. Wednesday's program, for example, has included a symposium on the Influence of Folk Music on Cello Literature, a discussion of Cello Music from China, Music on Jewish Themes, a workshop on Jazz Improvisation, a film, a master-class taught collectively by Janos Starker, the Honorary President of the Congress, and Greenhouse, its Artistic Advisor.

The evening's concert, in Joseph Meyerhoff Symphony Hall, has featured two young musicians, Wendy Warner—in her twenties—and the teen-aged Han-Na Chang. After intermission, and to thunderous applause, Yo-Yo Ma and the Baltimore Symphony Orchestra perform a new composition, "The Six Realms" by Peter Lieberson, and Tchaikovsky's "Andante Cantabile Op. 11." Then comes the usual post-concert line of well-wishers and then a bus-trip for invited guests to a reception on a cruise ship in the harbor. The bus driver, however, gets lost; the ship proves difficult to find, tucked into a dark corner of the marina, and by the time the cruise begins it is well past midnight. Dutifully, drinking jug-wine and decaffeinated coffee, the cellists and their sponsors make slow circles in the harbor while the engines thrum and mutter and the lights over Baltimore dim.

Janos Starker and Bernard Greenhouse, the Honorary President and the Artistic
Advisor of the World Cello Congress, on-stage in a shared "Master Class."

On the bus-trip back to Towson University, where
the musicians have been lodged, Greenhouse invites
Yo-Yo Ma to his room. Ma is gracious and respectful
and, it seems, indefatigable; the night before he had
been visiting late with Starker; in a few hours he must
leave for New York, but this cello commands his attention and he and Ko Iwasaki appear in Greenhouse's
suite. Ma carries his tail-coat over his arm; his dress-
shirt and black pants seem casual now, and he's sweat-
ing lightly in the late spring heat. With a flourish,
unlocking its case, the elder man produces his beloved
"Paganini Strad."

"It's 2:30 in the morning of Thursday, June 1, 2000, and three cellists are fondling a scroll." Ko Iwasaki, Bernard Greenhouse and Yo-Yo Ma at the World Cello Congress.

"Beautiful," says Yo-Yo Ma.

"Sensational," Iwasaki repeats.

"Here." Greenhouse proffers a bow.

The virtuoso demurs. Shaking his head, eyes narrowed behind wire-rimmed glasses, Ma studies the cello front and back, then plucks the strings and commences to play pizzicato. Iwasaki claps. After some time Ma takes the bow and — "Noodle a little," Greenhouse urges — plays a few notes lightly, dreamily, so as not to wake the sleeping guests. I ask him what he's hunting, what he listens for, and he says: the things it's easy to do, the things that are hard. It is three o'clock by now, and the men forget their resolution to be circumspect. "You should *hear* it," Greenhouse says. "Full-throated, down by the bridge."

Iwasaki excuses himself and collects his own cello, then returns to the room. He too possesses a "Strad," dated 1727, but this is a copy — one of six he has commissioned from the craftsman Timothy Jansma. This is Iwasaki's favorite copy, the one he has brought to the Congress — and the men measure proportion, dimension, comparing the two instruments. They talk of other cellos, other makers, other performers. What they do not talk

5

about—though the Stanlein, if sold, would fetch millions of dollars—is price. Yo-Yo Ma keeps caressing the cello's scroll, and when I ask him what's the word for what this instrument possesses he says, *"Gravitas."*

$$\int$$

ON SEPTEMBER 22, 1998, THE CELLIST BERNARD Greenhouse drove from his home in Massachusetts the five hours to Manhattan. On the car's rear seat reposed his prized possession, named in honor of two of its previous owners: the "Countess of Stanlein *ex*-Paganini" Stradivarius violoncello of 1707. Strapped and secure in its carrying case, the instrument traveled wherever he went, and it had done so for years. This afternoon, however, he was planning to realize a long-deferred dream and deposit the "Strad" in New York.

It did require work. There were nicks and scratches scattered on the surface, front and back. The varnish had roughened and darkened in spots; in others the varnish had thinned. Some previous patches needed retouching; in places the edging had cracked. The glue by the sound-post—an old repair—leaked. Decades of pressure on the neck and from the downward force of the bridge-feet beneath the taut-stretched strings had forced the f-holes into less than perfect symmetry; the ribs would need to be adjusted and the front plate aligned.

Not all of this was visible, and only the discerning eye would notice or, noticing, object. The instrument had long been famous for both its beauty and tone. But Greenhouse is a perfectionist, and previous repairs had been stop-gap and partial, in the service of utility. At the height of his career he performed—with the Bach Aria Group, as a founding member of the Beaux Arts Trio, as soloist and on recordings—nearly two hundred times per year. From continent to continent, in all sorts of weather and playing conditions the Countess of Stanlein had been his companion; he carried her on boats and planes, in rented cars and taxicabs and trains, and always in a rush.

Now the career was winding down. No longer appearing routinely in concert, he owned several other instruments to practice on at home. At eighty-two, the cellist

With Pablo Casals in 1946 at the Villa Collette, Casals's home in exile in the village of Prades.

had the money and unscheduled time and the desire to "give back," as he put it, "something of value" to the world of music that had given him so much. This was to be, he reasoned, both a good deed and investment; he knew just the man to do the job — René Morel, on West 54th St. — and the work had been agreed upon and delivery date arranged.

Greenhouse had been a student of the late Pablo Casals. After the Second World War he traveled to Prades, in the French Pyrenees, where the Catalan cellist lived in retirement. As a protest against Generalissimo

8

Franco, Casals accepted no public engagements but continued, in private, to work at his craft; there, in the church of Saint-Michel de Cuxa, he recorded the six Unaccompanied Suites for Violoncello by Johann Sebastian Bach. There too in 1946 he took on the young American as an apprentice. More than a half century later, that audition stays vivid for Greenhouse:

"Then he started asking for the repertoire, and he requested many pieces. After an hour or more of my playing—during which he indicated nothing more than the piece and the passage he wanted me to play—he said, 'All right. Put down your cello, put it away, and we'll talk.' He said to me, 'Well, what you need is an apprenticeship to a great artist. I believe in the apprentice system. Stradivarius, Guarnerius, Amati: they turned out so many wonderful violin makers. And I believe the same thing can hold true in making musicians. If I knew of a great artist I could send you to, I would do so,' he said, 'because my mind is very much occupied with the Spanish Republican cause. But since I don't know whom to send you to—and if you agree to stay in the village and take a lesson at least once every two days—I will teach you.'"

Such a system of tutelage remains in place today: implicit in the idea of "master classes" and explicit in the trade of the luthier. This is a generic term for those who make and repair bowed stringed instruments, and the enterprise feels nearly medieval in its hierarchy of apprentice, journeyman laborer, master craftsman. Young men still clean the varnish rags or sweep wood shavings from the floor as did their predecessors centuries ago, and under much the same close watchful supervision. Bernard Greenhouse met René Morel in the early 1950's when the luthier was working for the legendary Fernando Sacconi in the New York shop of Rembert Wurlitzer; he commended the Frenchman thereafter to the dealer Jacques Français. In 1990 Morel struck out on his own, both as dealer and restorer. His long and narrow studio is chockablock with wood and tools and work-in-progress on benches; his public rooms display memorabilia—signed concert posters and photographs of virtuosi—from the storied past.

What the luthier sells are violins and violas and cellos and bows of value and importance and what he repairs is the *crème de la crème*. There are workaday instruments also; nearly a thousand pass through his shop each year for sale or repair. A dealer's reputation, however, rests on the highest not lowest common denominator of stock, and to have handled "The Countess of Stanlein" is no small professional thing. Greenhouse and Morel admire each other cordially; they praise each other lavishly; they trust each other a little, and when the cellist delivered his cello for the purpose of "restoration" he left with a two by three inch numbered ticket as receipt.

$$\int$$

THE HUMAN ANIMAL MAKES LISTS. INSTINCTIVELY WE scan the charts for those who come first, second, last. We like to know the names of the ten best-or worst-dressed celebrities, the all-time all-star baseball team, the richest men or women and twelve safest cities for family life and the millennium's five or five hundred most important citizens. We rank colleges and wines. In our obsessive calibration of achievement by degrees,

there are tables and annotated lists of lists; it sometimes
seems as though the need to establish a "top dog" or
"leader of the pack" stays programmed in the species.
Hierarchy has its comforts, after all; we want to know
where we belong and, by extrapolation, where we stand.

Such ranking in terms of artistic achievement is a
thankless task. We may have heavyweight champions of
the world and world leaders in automobile or oil production, but enter the domain of art and any assess-
ment of primacy falls flat. Pick the "greatest" of
composers and for every proponent of Bach there'll be
a Beethoven buff; urge Mozart as the supreme musical
consciousness and you'll find an adept of Stravinsky
and one of Schubert or Schumann and one of Paul
Simon or Sting. Pick the "greatest" of visual artists and
there'll be votes cast in that beauty contest for Raphael
and Rembrandt and Da Vinci and Durer and Grandma
Moses and Andy Warhol and Monet. Even Shakespeare
has detractors: those who would put him in context or
claim that he couldn't be Shakespeare or prefer Milton
instead. The marketplace requires multiplicity, and to
insist that X outrank Y is to reveal mere personal pref-
erence or a set of cultural blinders; a declension of the

hundred "best books" or "all time favorite" love songs seems on the face of it inane.

For there can be no argument — no instructive disagreement — as to taste. *De gustibus non est disputandum* is a dictum accepted by all. Yet ask a hundred people to name the greatest of wooden stringed instrument makers, and ninety-five will agree. One name is preeminent, and those who challenge his reputation do so as iconoclasts. If you have heard of anyone you will have heard of Stradivari, and to propose Guadagnini or Gofriller or members of the Amati family as the most accomplished of luthiers is to lodge a protest as well as minority vote. (Guarneri "del Gesù" has his consequential advocates, and there are cognoscenti who prize his violins above all other instruments, but he died young and worked at speed and built, it would seem, only one cello.) I know of no artist or craftsman more universally honored than is Stradivari; his violins, violas and violoncellos have long been celebrated as and will in all likelihood remain the Platonic ideal of the form.

$$\int$$

ANTONIO STRADIVARI WAS BORN IN OR NEAR CREMONA,
Italy, in 1644. The actual date and place of his birth have
been lost, but various Stradivaris had prospered in
Cremona for centuries before. (The Latin and Italian
spelling of his patronymic — Stradivarius and Stradivari
— are interchangeable; by convention the former refers
to an instrument, the latter to its maker, but this is a distinction long-since blurred. Indeed, the proper orthog-
raphy was "Stradiuarius" until in 1730 the luthier
himself replaced the "u" with a roman "v." One of his vio-
lin-building sons retained it; another returned to the
"u.") Ottolinus Stradivari had been a *senator patriae* as
early as 1127; in 1186 there was a senator named Egidius
Stradivari; the lawyer Guglielmus Stradivertis died in
1439. In the sixteen thirties and forties, however, bubonic
plague swept through Cremona, and those who could
afford to do so departed to the countryside; during
plague years record-keeping was in any case at risk.

We know a good deal about the instrument maker
nevertheless, and this itself attests to prominence. *Ricco
come Stradivari* was a saying of the Cremonese vernacu-
lar, and it referred not to inheritance but earnings. He
did well. The great luthier lived long and was proud of

longevity; in 1736 he inscribed a violin now called the "Muntz" Stradivarius with a label in his own hand, claiming to be ninety-two years old. (His first such label, in which he describes himself as a pupil of Amati, was signed in 1666.) So our knowledge of the birth-date is in effect retrospective, a matter of subtraction, and whether he was born in Cremona or Brescia or Bergamo remains, as of this writing, moot.

He worked till the day of his death, and that day *was* recorded. *"In the year of our Lord one thousand seven hundred and thirty-seven, on the nineteenth day of the month of December, Signor Antonio Stradivari, a widower, aged about ninety-five years, having died yesterday, fortified by the Holy Sacraments and comforted by prayers for his soul until the moment he expired, I, Domenico Antonio Stancari, Parish Priest of this Church of S. Matteo, have escorted today his corpse with funeral pomp to the Church of the very Reverend fathers of S. Domenico in Cremona, where he was buried."* [1]

We think that we know what he looked like—tall, dark, fine-fingered—although there's no authenticated likeness; we're told he wore a white cap routinely, and a

15

The supposed portrait of Stradivari—more probably a
portrait of the composer Monteverdi.

white leather apron at work. We believe that he was
pious, self-effacing, not litigious. These qualities, however, are more a function of evidence absent than pre-
sent; for so long-lived and prosperous a citizen to have
engaged in so few court proceedings must mean he
stayed contentedly at home and in his shop. Lately his
testament has been unearthed; we know the size of his
estate—in a word, considerable—and what he distrib-

A line drawing of the house of Stradivari, No. 1,
Piazza Roma, now demolished.

uted where. The dates of his two marriages have been
recorded—to Francesca Ferraboschi, a widow and,
when he in turn became a widower, to Antonia
Zambelli—then the names of his children, their birth
dates, and which of them grew up.

We deduce from the signed label (*"Antonius
Stradiuarius fecit, Alumnus Nicolaiis Amati, Faciebat
Anno 1666"*) that he was apprenticed to Nicolo

17

René Morel in his workshop, holding a Stradivarius violin.

Amati. We assume he lived as well as plied his trade at Piazza Roma, #1. It's probable he hung his instruments to dry in the attic of that building, but the structure no longer exists. As is the case with Shakespeare, the provincial place that harbored him appeared at first indifferent; his bones were removed from the crypt of the church when the church itself was razed; his workshop too was leveled and his tools and patterns dispersed. Now Cremona celebrates its honored resident and ancient cottage industry; there's a museum of the violin, a festival devoted to violin making, and a tourism boom.

$\int$

RENÉ MOREL'S HAIR IS WHITE AND CURLY, HIS FIGURE trim in a blue smock, and he rolls back his shirtsleeves meticulously and sports a close-barbered moustache. In his late sixties, Gallic and dapper, the luthier maintains his eleventh-floor workshop in New York's theater district. Outside the locked glass door of his studio young dancers and singers rehearse, and he eyes them where they cluster in the hall. Those girls are wearing dental floss, not even a G-string, he says. *Ces jeunes gens là*, he says, they entertain me with their dream of entertainment; they have no idea at all how hard one has to work.

He himself, he says, works very hard; his father and grandfather made instruments and he himself has been elected President of the *Entente Internationale des Maîtres Luthiers et Archetiers d'Art* — Violin and Bow-makers. His assistants call him *Maître*, and he reports with pride that long ago Pablo Casals called him *Maître* Morel. He had been taken to the hotel where the famed artist was staying, then introduced as the young man who would "save" the cello Casals was to perform on that night. "And Sascha (Alexander Schneider) says, he's young but you'll see what he can do for you; so Casals comes up and Martita his wife was with him. I turned red, yellow, and he called me *Maître* Morel. I was looking for a mousehole to hide in, I shook, I was very much in awe and I said, oh,

Maestro Casals if you call me *Maître* then how may I address you? 'You must call me Pablo,' he says."

In Morel's own atelier — its proper name is Morel & Gradoux-Matt Inc., since in January 1999 he made a Swiss luthier his equal partner — dozens of instruments wait for repair. They range from the amateur's hand-me down "cigar-box" to the professional's ideal of excellence. In the former case he lets his assistants do the work, murmuring *"Bien"* if he approves or pointing out in no uncertain terms what needs to be redone. In the latter instance — when the instrument is of particular interest or of particular value — he does the work himself. And restoration, it's worth repeating, differs from repair. Repair may be accomplished rapidly — a small adjustment of bridge or sound-post in time for a concert, a brief application of glue and a clamp. But what he and Greenhouse contracted to do, within the limits of the possible, was full-fledged restoration, and this must be done with the instrument open, requiring patience and skill.

"When I was young," says Morel, "I could work twelve, fifteen hours at a time and never once be tired; my eyes were better then. But when you deal with

The Countess of Stanlein
ex-Paganini Stradivarius violoncello of 1707.

(*Left to right*)
Top (front) of cello.
Side-view of cello.
Rear (back) of cello.

restoration it cannot be hurried, it must not be rushed. To start with, we take it apart. Even so fine a lady as the Countess of Stanlein must be opened for examination; you insert the knife carefully, carefully just here into the glue — you must know how to do it — and then you just go *pop*!"

$$\int$$

WHAT ARE THE COMPONENTS OF THIS RESONAT-ING box; what kind of wood is it made of and in what proportion? If this truly represents the Platonic ideal of the form of a violoncello, then how may we best measure it and who established shape? Here's a skeletal description of the instrument's anatomy:

The top (alternatively called the *table, front plate* or *belly*) is by tradition made of two pieces of matching spruce or pine glued together. Two f-holes—so called because of their shape — are carved on the top of the instrument on each side; these are the apertures through which the sound of the vibrating plates is produced. The inside of the top is graded from 3/16 inches in the middle to 9/64 inches at the edges, for a cello with a body length of 29 inches.

The back is usually made of two matching pieces of maple — a harder wood than spruce or pine — selected for the figuration in and pattern of the wood. The back itself is graded from 4/16 inches at the center to 9/64 inches at each edge. (Stradivari did not, of course, work in inches, but by convention in the English-speaking world these measurements are registered as such.) A few cellos exist with one-piece backs. The *neck*, *scroll* and *peg box* also were originally shaped from one piece of maple. The necks of older cellos were shorter than today's, but because of the rise in pitch over the centuries, new, longer necks have had to be attached. When this is done, the peg box and scroll, an ornamental gesture on the part of the luthier, are retained if possible and replaced on the new neck.

There are *sides*, or *ribs* — six pieces of maple glued to the top and the back; there's a strip of light-colored wood glued between two strips of black wood to form

one tripartite strip. This is called *purfling*, and six of
these strips fit into a groove near the edge of each plate
for purposes of decoration; too, they protect the plate's
edge. There's an elaborately carved piece of light-
weight maple called a *bridge*; its feet are set — not
glued — between the f-holes, centered on the f-hole
notches, and it supports the four strings.

Over time such functional ornaments as an *endbutton*, a *nut* and *tailpiece* have become standard component parts of the instrument also; the endbutton is a
small, rounded piece of wood inserted into the end-
block with the cord of the tailpiece wrapped around it
and a hole bored through the middle for a metal end-
pin. That endpin is adjustable, raising the instrument
to its desired height and attaching to the floor. The
carved, triangular *tailpiece* is intended to keep the
strings taut. The *nut*, slightly higher than the fingerboard, is a small piece of ebony glued onto the neck
with grooves for proper spacing for the strings.

Interior component parts include the *linings*, the *bass
bar* and *sound post*. The linings consist of twelve narrow
strips of pine glued to the edges of the sides in order to
increase the surface to which the top and back plates will

be glued. The *bass bar* must be cut to fit the curvature of the top, then glued to the inside of the top on the left-hand side — where the lowest of the four strings, the C-string, is positioned; therefore the bar is called "bass." The *sound post* is not glued, placed just in front of the right foot of the bridge, with ends shaped exactly to fit the interior contours of the top and back; it transmits the vibration from plate to plate and its placing or adjustment is crucial to the sound produced.[2]

The end purpose of all such arrangements is, of course, sonority. Too heavy an instrument fails to respond; too light will sound tinny or thin. Issues of weight and volume and proportion have to do with both the quality and quantity of noise produced. The relatively slender walls of a guitar, for instance, will necessarily yield a different kind of vibration than those of a cello; sound-waves result from density as well as the wood's shape.

∫

I AM THE CELLIST'S SON-IN-LAW; I HAVE KNOWN HIM well by now for more than thirty years. In that time I have not known him to be separated from the instrument for more than a few weeks, when repair became imperative, and during that time—though playing on a copy he had commissioned from the luthier Martin Cornellisen—he was restless. He admires the Cornellisen, as well as other instruments he owns (in particular a Contreras, known as the "Spanish Stradivarius"), but The Countess of Stanlein is his heart's darling, his pearl among white peas . . .

As with many other performers, stories attach to the matter of attachment: how Greenhouse lost the cello once, in transit, on a plane to Paris and found it in Vienna on the airport tarmac; how he left it in a taxi in Dubrovnik, and spent a sleepless night because the cabbie, once identified, said he himself required sleep and would return the cello in the morning; how he braved a machine-gun wielding Customs Inspector in South America who wanted to subject the instrument to a strip search. (When Yo-Yo Ma misplaced his Montagnana in a New York taxi's trunk two years ago, its loss became a cause célèbre and its recovery a cause for celebration. Now his recorded voice inside the cab offers passengers

COURTESY KLM ROYAL DUTCH AIRLINES

"In early days of airplane travel, the Countess of Stanlein could come along free." Bernard Greenhouse, Menahem Pressler and Daniel Guilet of The Beaux Arts Trio aboard "The Flying Dutchman" in the late 1950's.

the "classical advice" to remember their belongings
once the ride is done.)

In early days of airplane travel, the Countess of
Stanlein could come along free; then a "companion"
ticket would be issued at half-price, ("How old is your
son Cello, Mr. Greenhouse?" an official in Newark
once asked.) Then, with the increase in airplane traffic
and procedural regulation, the cello's ticket became
full-fare — it cannot, of course, be stowed in the hold —
and now the instrument must travel in isolated splen-
dor, strapped into its own wide padded seat in first
class. The Russian soloist, Raya Garbousova, claimed to
have avoided that expensive inconvenience by calling
her cello a "bass balalaika" and, because airplane reg-
ulations made no mention of that instrument, she carried her "Strad" at no cost . . .

All such association entails accommodation, and
habit entails a resistance to change. Since this musician and his cello have been inseparable for decades,
the performer and instrument fuse. Less a romantic
vagary than statement of fact, such a process is familiar to any practiced maker or player; the idiosyn-
crasies of an instrument, perplexing to "A," will

The virtuoso Raya Garbousova with her "bass balalaika" in 1948.

become second nature to "B." And Morel knows how Greenhouse reacts:

"He was so fixed on the bridge Maestro Sacconi had cut for him that he wouldn't let it be moved. You ask him if I'm lying, it's probably been there now for thirty years and we spent fifteen years without moving the sound-post either; of all my customers this is the one who has remained the longest with the same material. But Bernie, when he was younger and I first heard him play, he and his cello were one and one only; I always say there is no one in the world who could master that sound, it's *his* sound with the cello; you give that cello to anybody else and it won't sound the same. He has a way with the flesh of the finger, the vibrato of the hand — I was flabbergasted and I said to myself, that's it, that's the complete sound of this instrument, the player and the instrument are one."

The luthier's task, therefore, is twofold: to restore the physical object and not by the act of restoration to change the instrument's sound. This is a delicate balancing act, all the more so when musician and cello have been long-standing intimates; unnumbered hours in rehearsal and performance make a millimeter's difference in the height of the bridge or the width of the neck loom large. Greenhouse knows as if by instinct how to produce his particular tone; he and his instrument are — as Morel says admiringly — "one."

$$\int$$

"THE CITY OF CREMONA, CAPITAL OF THE PROVINCE of the same name, is of great antiquity, having been founded by the Romans in the year 218 B.C . . . .Whether or not Cremona is distinguished as the actual scene of the emergence of the true violin by the hands of Andrea Amati, founder of the Cremona School, or whether that honor should belong to the neighboring city of Brescia, where Gasparo da Salo also fashioned instruments of violin form in the sixteenth century, the significance of Cremona will ever remain of first magnitude in the story of the Violin."[3]

So writes Ernest Doring in the impressively titled: *How Many Strads? Our Heritage From the Master; A*

Tribute to the Memory of a Great Genius, compiled in the year marking the Tercentenary of his birth; being a Tabulation of Works Believed to Survive Produced in Cremona by Antonio Stradivari, Between 1666 and 1737, including relevant data and mention of his two sons Francesco and Omobono.

To return to the matter of "first magnitude" and ranking, it's no small mystery that this small town in the north of Italy should have provided the locus for so many of the world's important bowed wooden instruments. There are some who claim it was a function of the excellence of available timber — much of it shipped across the Adriatic; there are some who argue for the town apothecary and the varnish he produced; there are others who attribute this "genius of place" to the system of apprenticeship as such. Roughly between the latitudes of 44 and 46 degrees, from west of Milan to Venice and Udine (although the luthier David Tecchler lived in Rome and the Gagliano family in Naples), a group of craftsmen prospered. Andrea and Nicolo Amati, Francesco Ruggeri, Andrea Guarneri were working in Cremona before Stradivari was born; Guarneri "del Gesù," Carlo Bergonzi, Lorenzo Storioni and G.B. Ceruti — this list is truncate, selective — continued after his death.

Most likely, of course, there is no single answer but a confluence of answers to the question: why then and why there? The quality of wood and varnish, the nature of apprenticeship and exigencies of competition would each have played a role. But whatever the reason or reasons, in the seventeenth and eighteenth centuries a skill came to fruition in and near Cremona that has not been equaled since. Although genius itself may be neither explicable nor replicable, that part of the luthier's art which can be called pure craftsmanship can be in part transmitted — rather like the guild of stone-workers, the Cosmati, who set the floors of churches and crypts with intricate inlaid geometrical patterns, then watched their trade die off.

This trade, however, thrives. More people play wooden stringed instruments more widely now than ever before; there's a flourishing business both in construction and repair. The membership directory of The American Federation of Violin and Bow Makers (1998-1999) lists members from Ames to Zygmuntowicz with offices from Arizona to Wisconsin. René Morel's workshop in

Manhattan contains no native English speakers but a poly-
glot transient or resident crew; his assistants speak
Japanese, French, German, and Czech. Today the business
is international, not local, and performers cross borders
habitually; there's no fixed center of the music-making
world. Yet the young luthier still travels to Cremona as a pil-
grim to a holy place and, in the museum where the master's tools and patterns and drawings and instruments have
been reassembled, still visits as though at a shrine.

For a few years the "Cremonese" were eclipsed—at
the turn of the nineteenth century German instruments
outranked the Italians in terms of purchase price—but
ever since then, in Jane Austen's phrase, "it is a truth
universally acknowledged, that a single" music lover "in
possession of a good fortune must be in want of" an
instrument built in that time and place. And, if he or she
be very rich or skilled or fortunate indeed, the instrument will likely come from Stradivari himself.

$$\int$$

HERE IS GREGOR PIATIGORSKY REPORTING ON THE BATTA
Stradivarius violoncello of 1714. "I played the 'Batta' for
a long time before appearing in concert with it. In soli-
tude, as is befitting honeymooners, we avoided inter-
fering company until then. From that day on, when I
proudly carried the 'Batta' across the stage for all to
greet, a new challenge entered into my life. While all
other instruments I had played prior to the 'Batta' dif-
fered one from the other in character and range, I knew
their qualities, shortcomings, or their capriciousness
enough to exploit their good capabilities to full advantage. Not so with the 'Batta,' whose prowess had no lim-
itations. Bottomless in its resources, it spurred me on
to try to reach its depths, and I have never worked
harder or desired anything more fervently than to draw
out of this superior instrument all that it has to give.
Only then will I deserve to be its equal." [4]

$\int$

"THIS IS NOT MY BIGGEST RESTORATION," SAYS MOREL. "I have done much more difficult work than this, I have restored instruments that were considered garbage — when I was in my thirties there was no challenge I wouldn't take. When I heard Maestro Greenhouse play, while I was still at Wurlitzer, his sound always moved me; it wasn't the largest sound, but whenever he touched the string it was unforced. He is very much a perfectionist, very much a serious person, the same way he is with his music — he used to bring me the cello once a year to deal with the cracks and all that, and he said, someday, René, you will work with this cello and restore it entirely. And I said it would be an honor for me one day to work for you. And now that he wants his cello preserved, it is with this in mind that I am doing it. He's going to get my best," — the luthier spreads his hands and lifts his arms and shoulders — "not the second best."

A major challenge, for example, has to do with varnish—worn away since Stradivari's time and inexpertly replaced. The luthier shakes his head and points to blackened patches where, he says, his predecessors went *slap, slap,* and *drip.* Morel removes these accretions with pure denatured alcohol and a small sable retouching brush. Very carefully he paints the alcohol across the grain with two, three, or four strokes of the brush; he repeats this gesture often enough to soften the surface of the varnish but not enough to go through. Then he removes the loose new varnish with a scraper or sharp knife.

To take off all such coating requires, of course, that Morel distinguish between the varnish Stradivari used and that which has been added since 1707. "It's not only the eyes," he tells me, "but also the feeling, the texture of the varnish, and the minute the original comes up you know that that is it." The varnish on the cello's back is almost wholly original, and so is the coloration of the scroll. But the varnish of the top had been much retouched, as well as darkened by the natural oils of the performer's hand, and when I ask Morel—pointing to an area of two-square inches by the f-hole—how long it will take to clean this particular surface to his own satisfaction he says he cannot count how many days, it's one of the difficult jobs.

"Bernie says to me—I used to call him Mister Greenhouse, Maestro Greenhouse, but then he says, no, you must call me by the name my friends use, *Bernie* — make sure René you're the one to do this, because you have to know when to stop. If *you* put a drop of alcohol on that Strad varnish it will go to the white in no time, so you ask me, how can I use alcohol here? If *you* play the instrument and ask Bernie how much pressure do you put on the bow, he will raise his shoulders and shrug; if a virtuoso is going to play a concerto and he doesn't have the strings in tune, then he shouldn't attempt the concerto. I use alcohol, pure alcohol. And the answer to how to do it is skill. Skill, experience, feelings and concentration."

$$\int$$

WINDOWS LINE THE WORK-ROOM OF MOREL & GRADOUX-Matt Inc.; unsheathed lamps increase the light. The room is narrow, high-ceilinged and long; its shelves stock a jumble of shapes. Seventeen violins hang from a rack; there are dismembered instruments and cardboard boxes full of wood beneath the cluttered tables where the men bend to their work.

They are in their twenties and thirties, convivial yet focused; they sport ponytails and paint-bespattered T-shirts and smell of resin, tobacco and sweat. They rasp and sand and join and splice; they use clamps and calipers and scrapers and chisels and fine-pointed brushes and rags. There are boxes of spruce scraps, boxes of necks—labeled in black capital letters: CELLO, VIOLIN—a band saw, a poster of a Ferrari, cans of neck-graft, dental compound, rabbit glue, jam-jars labeled "chicory" and "potassium dichromate" with which they will varnish "white" wood. The radio plays. I expect to hear Haydn, Vivaldi perhaps—but what these craftsmen listen to is rock-and-roll, a D.J. selling cameras and Reeboks and reporting on the weather and traffic tie-ups in New Jersey.

Morel walks through. He moves from desk to desk, assistant to assistant, examining their labors' progress, joking about masking tape and how I will steal his trade secrets. Half the work we do, he tells me, is to repair what had been badly done in other shops; invisible mending, that's what we're after here. When it looks very bad, he says, it's often not so serious, and when it's very serious it's not always easy to see. He points to a patch near the sound-post, newly fitted and glued into place. Each cut begins with a saw in order, as Morel explains, "to approximate dimension. Then we use knives and rasps to remove most of the wood, and then we get the shape, and then after this we use files and in the end scrapers for very thin shavings. And then sandpaper, and after sandpaper we wet the wood three times because when you wet the wood the grain rises, and it must be sanded back . . ."

$$\int$$

ALTHOUGH THE VIOLIN AND VIOLONCELLO HAVE CHANGED their shapes with time—in the former case a little, in the latter quite considerably—the pattern as such remains fixed. I mean by "pattern" here the quintessence of form and not its surface adjustment; the cello's functional proportions were no doubt determined by trial and error, and that process continues today. Routinely some someone claims to have discovered the "secret" of a Stradivarius and to reproduce its excellence in plastic or metal or by computer; routinely that someone is wrong. We may play electronic cellos, ergonomically friendly cellos, reduced or outsize cellos, but these are understood as variations on a theme. (The change in the structure of bows is a separate but related subject; the *beau idéal* of a Tourte bow stands in much the same relation to the run-of-the-mill version thereof as does a Stradivarius to a factory-issue machine.) And it's no doubt the case that contemporary instruments could "season" with age, sounding more impressive to the listener in three hundred years. Wood is a natural substance; it alters over time.

Still, the art and craft of the luthier attained its height in Cremona, and most modern practitioners attempt to imitate not alter that ideal. It's as though Cezanne or Kandinsky sought only to paint in the manner of Titian or Brueghel, as though the contemporary writer tried only to write like the Greeks. For all practical purposes this fidelity to the ancient mode of instrument production remains the test of excellence, and I know no other métier of which this can be said. Singers, athletes, architects each profit from the new technologies; they take advantage of modern techniques. The luthier too deploys fiberglass molds and new chemical compounds and fine-tuned calipers and ultrasound for instrument repair. But the aim is reproduction, not innovation, and the model is a constant one.

This is, of course, a debatable point. The luthier Joseph Curtin of Ann Arbor, Michigan, states the alternative position succinctly and well. "By way of counterexample there is a small but significant number of highly qualified makers engaged in a far more ambitious project than reproduction. Remember too that many contemporary makers, makers not specially committed to innovation, are still doing a fine job of putting their own stamp on the craft, which is all that any maker after Andrea Amati—assuming he invented the violin—can claim. Whenever the next genius comes along, his or her work will stand on its own terms and create a new set of paradigms . . . The success of such innovation should be judged not by looking back over our shoulders to Cremona, but in terms of how well they both meet the needs of musicians and satisfy our own evolving sense of tonal beauty."[5]

Until that "next genius comes along," however, we
retain as paradigm the "innovation" of the Cremonese.
To produce such an object today would be to scale the
heights of achievement; to equal that old mastery is the
best that can be wished. Composers make new music,
sculptors new sculpture and carriage makers new cars
— but a Stradivarius in private home or symphony hall
remains the practitioner's dream. For performer and
audience both, in the nature of their handling or the
volume and quality of sound produced, in terms of aes-
thetics or acoustics these bowed wooden instruments
have neither been improved upon nor by technology
rendered obsolete.

Yet an instrument unplayed is an instrument ill-served.
The use to which it should be put is audible, and over
centuries such usage entails stress: material fatigue. It's
not like a text which, printed, remains constant or a paint-
ing which, once framed, needs only to be seen. Fingers
press on it; flesh brushes it; jewelry and liquor hover
nearby, poised to scratch or spill; humidity alters from
venue to venue and from day to day. The concert cellist
who performs in Rio de Janeiro on Monday, in Seoul the
next week and in London next month subjects his instru-

ment as well as himself to continuous wear and tear. The glue will dry, the joinings split, the wood itself will splinter and the ornamental strips of purfling crack and the varnish fade. Inattentive or ignorant handling, a car-crash or train-wreck or water or fire: such threats are omnipresent and everything's at risk. Strings, bridges, end-pins, sound-posts — each sooner or later requires attention and must be replaced.

$$\int$$

MOREL IS A BORN RACONTEUR AND HE LIKES TO TELL stories of contests of skill; the style includes rodomontade. "I never had to work on commercial instruments; I had been trained in France, where my very first teacher was Marius Didier. He was seventy-two years old, and I was twelve years old, starting to make violins after school; later, in Mirecourt, I studied with *Maître* Amédée Dieudonne. So I developed skill for making violins in the old school of violin making, and in order to earn a living I had to make them at the rate of two violins — in the white, without varnish — per week. We had no machinery, not even an electric motor. This seems impossible now, but there are still people living who can assure you of that . . . And when I came to Wurlitzer I brought along my tools, and they came with the band-saw, and I said, well, you take your band-saw and I'll take my hand-saw and we'll see who finishes first. Also, who comes closer to the line, to the pattern. We didn't bet any money, but I won; I won out over the band-saw. In my life as a luthier I seldom saw anybody else who could manage that way; it sounds as if I'm bragging but I'm not, it's a true fact.

"When I arrived at Mr. Wurlitzer and presented myself to Maestro Sacconi — this I will never forget — he gave me a bridge to cut, for a violin, a Lupot. Maestro Sacconi spoke French, and he said, this violin is one of your compatriots, and this is the model I want you to cut, that's the one I like. So I gave him the new bridge maybe forty minutes later, and he said, Already? And I said, Yes, why not? So he looked at it, and I'll never forget his face, he said, 'My God!' Then he looked and looked and showed it to his right arm, D'Attili; they couldn't believe that I'd cut it with my knife, you know, and they came to look at my knife because they couldn't believe that I'd done it with no knife marks, so clean and exactly similar to the model. The next bridge he gave me was for a cello, and after I'd cut that one he said, 'Bravo!'

"I have had some difficulties, because I don't hide what I do. Some shops, they close their doors to the public; I don't. When I have been showing my colleagues they say what I am doing is too risky; it's risky when you don't know what you do. It's not risky when you do. This is what I mean when I compare myself to a surgeon: you know how to do one job, one thing, and you must do it entirely."

$\int$

THE ART OF INSTRUMENT MAKING IS A LONG-ESTABLISHED one. So too is the craft of repair. "In Saronno, Italy, a town about 20 miles north of Milan, a fresco on the inside of the dome above the chancel in the church of Santa Maria dei Miracoli pictures, among other figures, an angel dressed in a luminous blue robe, playing the cello, primitive though the instrument may be. The cello, along with the violin and viola that are also pictured, is of a natural wood color. The fresco, painted by Gaudenzio Ferrari in 1535–36, provides evidence that the cello emerged some time before 1535."[6]

The cello is, of course, neither the first nor last wooden stringed instrument to have made its appearance in Europe; its ancestors include the lute and viol as well as viola da gamba. Relatives include the violin, viola and guitar. Its proper name suggests a "little violon," or double-bass viol, since 'cello in Italian is a diminutive, and the first such instrument clearly referred to in print — by Jambe de Fer in 1556 — was a "violoncello da spalla." This refers to the manner of holding the instrument in church processionals or serenades. "Spalla" means shoulder in Italian, and the player could perform while walking; the short-necked instrument was hung across the shoulder and fastened with a strap. By the turn of the twentieth century it had grown customary to abbreviate the name "violoncello" to "'cello," with the apostrophe indicating the six missing letters. By now it's acceptable to use the name "cello" without apostrophe and as a full designation; I have done so here.

This change in nomenclature, moreover, suits the fluid nature of such history; alteration inheres in the craft. No "pure" Stradivarius violoncello exists. There are roughly sixty still extant, and each differs from the cello as at first designed. No matter how earnest the performance of a practitioner of "early music," what the Maestro once heard in his workshop is not what we, listening, hear. What we look at is not what he saw.

A legend attaches to "La Messie," the Stradivarius violin in Oxford's Ashmolean Museum, that it was rarely if ever performed upon, and there are many instruments housed elsewhere under glass. This has the virtue of preservation—of keeping an artifact out of harm's way—but the luthier's work had been, of course, intended to be played. And if form follows function, then the form must shift.

In the seventeenth century the literature was written for continuo (a bass-line repetition of the featured melody), but Boccherini and Bach and their successors wrote for solo instrument. This expansion of the repertoire and shift of emphasis required an equivalent increase in acoustic volume and a heightened pitch. The neck was lengthened and bridge raised and the fingerboard and interior bass-bar enlarged. In the nineteenth century traditional sheep-gut strings were wire-wrapped to augment the production of sound. The locus of performance also changed, enlarging into the auditorium, and an end-pin was added to provide stability and anchor the frame to the floor. Today the violoncellist — unlike soloists on the violin, viola or bass — must sit.

$\int$

HERE IS BERNARD GREENHOUSE ON HIS FIRST VIEWING of the instrument. It was not his first Stradivarius; he had previously owned the "Visconti da Madrona," a cello dated 1684 and in the "old pattern" (built up from the viola da gamba). That instrument — now owned by Mstislav Rostropovitch — had been "decorated," festooned with the Visconti coat

Greenhouse with luthier Joseph Settin, and the "Visconti da Madrona" Stradivarius violincello of 1684. The crest of the Visconti adorns the cello's back.

of arms in order to disguise its added wood. The cello's sound, however, did not project well or merge compatibly with that produced by Daniel Guilet, the founding violinist of the Beaux Arts Trio. Therefore Greenhouse had been, as he puts it, "in the market" and was in Europe on tour.

"In 1957, the instrument dealer, Jacques Français, said he thought there might be a cello available near Cologne, in the small city of Aachen, and that if I were ever in the neighborhood I might just take a look.

The Beaux Arts Trio with the composer Aaron Copeland standing at the piano, in rehearsal.

"It happened that I was playing a concert in Cologne, and we had a free afternoon, and so I took a train to Aachen, which the French know as Aix-la-Chapelle. I arrived at the station and looked in the telephone book for a *Geigenbauer* (the German term for a luthier), then took a taxi to his shop and told him I was an American cellist and had heard there was a Stradivarius in the area; did he know it and had he ever worked on it? The *Geigenbauer*,

53

Mr. Niessen, said by all means, yes. For many years it had been in the collection of a Mr. Talbot, who had died just recently, and his wife still had the instrument. I asked him to call the daughter and find out if I might look at the cello; soon afterwards a man arrived, and I opened the cello case and fell immediately in love. I had no doubt, no doubt at all that it was a Stradivarius; I didn't even look inside to find the label. The color of the varnish, the shape of the instrument, it was so beautiful, so very beautiful, and it seemed to me a great jewel ... "

$$\int$$

HOW DID THE CELLO REACH AACHEN; WHERE HAD IT BEEN before? It's not now possible to track the object throughout its lengthy provenance: who first commissioned or played it, how much it was valued by whom. There would be charm and drama in such telling —witness the movie, "The Red Violin," where we see a fabled instrument in various cultural contexts, from Italy to China, and passing through various hands. That film may well have been inspired by John Hersey's novel, *Antonietta*, in which the writer imagines a violin made by Stradivari while courting his second wife, Antonia Zambelli.

In both cases the dramatic problem is the same: how would this token of devotion be treated by musicians and collectors in the several centuries after having been created by a great luthier in love? In the film a nameless "Cremonese" mixes his dead darling's blood into the violin's varnish, and the instrument thereafter becomes an emblem of fatal romance. Hersey's plot is also episodic and sequential; he makes Mozart admire "Antonietta"; Berlioz and Stravinsky fall turn by turn under its spell, till it fetches up on Martha's Vineyard; thence the auction block . . .

Our information on "The Countess of Stanlein's" early history is finite but suggestive. We do know, for example, that "the late Count Stanlein" purchased it in 1854 from the French instrument maker and dealer, Jean-Baptiste Vuillaume (who was the foremost champion of "Cremonese" instruments in Paris at that time). Let's imagine for a moment that Count Stanlein (*à la*

Stradivari in *Antonietta*) was courting a wife. He would have commissioned a string quartet or perhaps have been an amateur himself, so the name is his high compliment to their anticipated harmony: a nuptial gift of song. This was the period when chamber-music, as the term indicates, was still a private matter; aristocrats routinely concertized at home. The Count's betrothed may well have sung or played the spinet and he would have desired to join her in the music-room as well as in the bed. It's less likely although possible the lady herself played the instrument, and "The Countess of Stanlein" refers to the musician who held it between her spread legs. There's a tell-tale splash of brandy on the rear plate of the cello, where the varnish bubbled and was—perhaps by her handkerchief or the hem of a raised silk undergarment—wiped clean.

Or perhaps Count Stanlein had no wife and fondled this substitute "Countess" instead. She would have been broad-beamed, deep-throated, her color reddish-gold. The instrument had previously been owned — witness the title, "ex-Paganini" — by that notorious rakehell and virtuoso who sold it to Vuillaume. Vuillaume himself was a celebrated copyist; his gift of imitation remains unsurpassed, and he built many cellos on the model of the Countess — her proportions having been, by the mid-nineteenth century, acknowledged as ideal.

It's tempting to imagine such a purchase and seduction, as Hersey did in his novel, or the film for "The Red Violin." But the actual story of its discovery and recovery is a good deal less romantic and has the ring of truth.

Here's what we do know of previous ownership, summarized dismissively by the brothers Hill. As historians of Stradivari, the Hill family — English dealers and instrument-makers — were, for many years, authoritative; their work remains fundamental to what is accepted today: " . . . The most interesting fact known to us concerning this instrument is the episode of its purchase early in the last century by Signor Merighi, a violoncellist of Milan, and Piatti's master. We have it on the authority both of Piatti and of Signor Pezze, also a pupil of Merighi, that in 1822, while the last-named was passing through the streets of Milan, he perceived a working man carrying, among other things, a violoncello on a truck or barrow. Merighi at once accosted him and ended by becoming the owner of the instrument, which was in a dilapidated state, for a sum equivalent to 4s! Eventually, about 1834–35, Merighi disposed of the 'cello to Paganini, who sold it to J.B. Vuillaume, who resold it in 1854 to the late Count Stanlein."[7]

$\int$

FROM 1707 TO 1822, THERE'S NO FORMAL RECORD of ownership and we can only guess at who played and disposed of it how. The notion of a cello "on a truck or barrow," broken apart and ready for the municipal dump — then at the last minute rescued by Merighi — has operatic flair. More probably the thing was being trundled from one owner or shop to another; most likely it wasn't at risk. But this did happen at a time, in the wake of the Napoleonic Wars, when instruments were subject to rough handling. The "violin hunter" Luigi Tarisio — himself in large part responsible for the rediscovery of the "Cremonese" masters — was said to have walked into Paris with his collec-

tion in a sack. He had acquired his treasures in the
north of Italy by just such wayward and wayside
encounter, finding instruments in attics and church
basements and the backs of barns . . .

So the Hill brothers' anecdote should be taken with a
grain if not fistful of salt. By contrast the certificate of
authenticity issued by the firm of Hamma & Co.,
Stuttgart, on 19 June 1949, rings with unstinting praise.
From the Stanlein family the cello would appear to have
been sold to Paul Grümmer of the Busch quartet, who
sold it to the Talbots, from whom in turn Greenhouse
acquired it in 1958. The certificate has photographs of the
top, the back, the scroll and then a description extolling
the virtues of the *"echt und zusammen-gehörend"* instrument, the *"Violoncello mit Originalzettel, Antonius
Stradiuarius Cremona 1707."* That "dilapidated state" of
which the Hills complain is gainsayed by the German
firm, which writes: "In all its essential parts a very
impressive Work of this Master; it is authentic and
belongs together . . . "

Still, not all the luthier's creations are equally
achieved. They were fashioned by hand and piece by
piece and with slight variations in wood and color

59

and shape. Little adjustments of size and proportion loom large in terms of acoustics; some instruments are forgiving and mellow, others harsh and stern. From 1680 to 1700 Stradivari produced at least thirty violoncellos, of which twenty-five survive, and they are without exception built of a large size (nearly thirty-two inches long, of an average, as opposed to 29 and a half.). Acoustically these instruments are an uneasy cross between bass viol and viola da gamba, and for seven years the workshop produced no documented cellos, then emerged in the "great period" — a designation propounded by the Hills — from 1707 to 1720.

The Stanlein comes from the first year of this resumed production, and thereafter the pattern stays more or less fixed. Why Stradivari's workshop should have curtailed the production of cellos from 1700 to 1707 is an intriguing question—with, once again, various answers. First, the instrument was just beginning to emerge from its subordinate performing role, and the demand might still have been small. More patrons would have asked for violins than violoncellos, and the instrument maker worked on commission and would

have complied. Second, its size requires labor dispro-
portionate to that entailed in the construction of violins; some three times the wood and work are necessary
for the larger object, and this has practical—which is to
say economic—consequences. There were several
other makers — Grancino, Gofriller and Techler
among them — whose proportional output of cellos is
greater than Stradivari's; they may well have "cor-
nered the market" till the market itself enlarged.

Or, plausibly, the master craftsman was dissatisfied
with the shape of his previous product and required some
time to refine it; we have no drawings or interim models
to confirm this, but it's clear that he made changes and that
the changes, once arrived at, satisfied both Stradivari and
his patrons. From 1707 to 1730 the model varied only a little, and for the thirteen years until 1720 it varied scarcely
at all. His masterpieces of the "great period" include such
other violoncellos as The Batta, the Davidov, the Duport,
the Gore-Booth and the Piatti. Often these were named for
those aristocrats who commissioned or the musicians
who performed on them; often for distinguishing charac-
teristics—as in instruments called the "blonde," (refer-
ring to varnish color, since the characteristic "Strad"

varnish of the period is a deep reddish-brown) or (his last violin) the "swan."

The Hills grow quasi-rhapsodic when writing of "that incomparable form of violoncello which time has taught us to accept as the *ne plus ultra* of perfection." They then proceed to describe perfection in terms that are pertinent here:

"The supreme merit of violoncellos of this type, irrespective of their beauty of form, their purity of style, and finished workmanship, consists in the exactitude of proportions, which in their *ensemble* produce a tone result but rarely — we may perhaps say never — found in any other instruments of the many and various Italian makers. They stand alone in representing the exact dimensions necessary for the production of a standard of tone which combines the maximum of power with the utmost refinement of quality, leaving nothing to be desired: bright, full and crisp, yet free from any suspicion of either nasal or metallic tendency . . .

"One is impressed by the general closeness of build, and the absence throughout of any superfluous wood; the interior blocks and linings are, for instance, of the smallest dimensions compatible with strength; the wood of the sides is planed as thin as possible, then, as a precaution against breakage; or more probably against the tendency to buckle, which is so often the case with the sides of Italian violoncellos, he reinforced them with small strips of canvas . . . "[8]

∫

THIS NOTION OF TRIAL AND ERROR — EXPERIMENTATION and innovation—is worth elaborating on. The reason Stradivari reinforced his instruments' ribs with "small strips of canvas" no doubt had to do with the width desired in order to magnify sound. Too thick a rib or too heavy a wood may dampen resonance; too thin or too light will be subject to breakage. The science of acoustics has grown more exact over time, but that most sensitive of calibrating instruments—the human ear—is being spoiled by background noise; the hum and buzz of machinery sounds omnipresent now. The maker in his shop in seventeenth century Cremona would not have known about wave theory or particle physics or directional tone color, but neither would he have had to contend with air conditioning or airplanes or the microphone. Even during Stradivari's lifetime they were refashioning his cello necks, and therefore to stay faithful to the originating impulse is to acknowledge an altered condition of playing and hearing. So what Morel embarks upon is in effect the restoration of an innovation: constancy in change.

"If I were to guess," writes Joseph Curtin, "in which direction the violin is trying to evolve, I would say, *in the same direction as it always has—toward a bigger sound.* The lower arching introduced by Stradivari and Guarneri, along with the modern bridge, bow, and set-up, have all tended to maximize power and focus. I believe this evolution will continue, if it can, because the forces which originally fuelled it — larger halls, the greater volume of its frequent accompanist, the piano, the competitive instincts of violinists — are still very much with us. Added to this, the recording industry has increased the pressure on players, I think, by raising listener expectation. Recordings allow, in exchange for a certain loss of "realism," a kind of intensity and presence to the sound that is almost completely lost in large halls. Recordings allow one to hear the violin not as it sounds in a hall, but as it sounds under the ear of the violinist . . .

"And though I am not an accomplished violinist, I love hearing what a great violin does under my ear, being fully aware that some important portion of this experience is inaccessible to the listener. It is part of a closed loop connecting player, bow, and instrument. But it is within this closed loop, I believe, that innovation in violinmaking will either succeed or fail."[9]

$$\int$$

HERE, AGAIN, IS BERNARD GREENHOUSE SPEAKING of his instrument: "The quality of sound is something that one wears, that adorns an individual as though it

Publicity photo for the 25 year old soloist in 1941.

Publicity photo for the "elder statesman," Greenhouse in 1998. Eighty-two and preparing to deliver the "Strad" to Morel.

were a beautiful piece of apparel. The ear can be
deceiving sometimes; sometimes I'll pick up one of the
lovely modern celli in the morning and be very happy
with it, but in the afternoon I'll ask what could possibly
have pleased me. The ear changes; if you sneeze, for
example, your hearing becomes clear and not pleas-
antly so; sometimes such a clarity is something you
don't want. So sound is not absolutely fixed, not
entirely a constant, but with my Strad there was never
a time when I've been disappointed. No matter the
weather or humidity, it stayed alive under my ear.

"There's a lusciousness about the sound. Under the
ear it's a little bit coarse but this turns to velvet out in
the hall, in the listener's ear. To the player there's an
ease of performance no modern instrument can equal;
the changes in the color of sound cannot be equaled.
Color of sound is produced on an instrument in three
manners; there are three elements to this, just as there
are three primary colors in the painter's palette. We
have the ability to place the bow closer to the bridge or
to the fingerboard, and that produces a particular
sound. In addition we have the speed of the bow, and
the speed of the bow produces more sound without

added pressure. That's the second primary color, and the third is the amount of effort we put into the bow. With those three primary colors we can produce an enormous variety of sound — analogous, again, to what a painter does with the palette."

$$\int$$

THE LUTHIER IS CONSCIOUS OF HIS CHALLENGE AND THE exacting intensity of his client, and the two of them consult on what can and cannot be done. At some point, for instance (most probably in the late eighteenth century), a workman cut away a rear section of the scroll so as to gain easy access to the peg-wound strings. Morel could plausibly have filled in the wood and reconstructed the scroll—but this has become a "signature" feature of the cello, and the two men opted for consistency. Too, the brandy-spill that marred the varnish of the back has been reduced but retained; it's part of the "Stanlein" lore, and traces of that bubbling indiscretion—an admirer of Paganini perhaps, a hovering lover of the Countess?—have been kept.

This holds equally true for another famous Stradivarius cello, the "Mara" bass. Once again we have this story from the brothers Hill: "The 'Mara' bass, made in the same year as the 'Duport,' strongly resembles it in character, work, and proportions, the model being a shade higher. Mara, husband of the celebrated singer of that name, appears to have been a man of dissolute habits and violent temper, and unfortunately his violoncello seems to have suffered somewhat from his viciousness. Traces of alcoholic liquor having been upset and allowed to drop from the top to the bottom sides, removing the beautiful varnish on its downward course, are still discernible. Whence Mara obtained this fine instrument is unknown."[10]

And here is Ernest Doring on the great Duport Stradivarius of 1711. "One day, while Duport was playing a solo at a private party at the Tuilleries, Napoleon suddenly appeared in the drawing room, booted and spurred. He listened with pleasure, and as soon as the piece was over he approached Duport, complimented him, and, snatching the bass from him with his usual vivacity, he asked, 'How the devil do you hold this, Monsieur Duport?' and, sitting down, he squeezed the poor violoncello between his spurred boots. The unfortunate artist, whom mingled respect and surprise had stricken dumb for a moment, could not master his fright at seeing his precious bass treated like a war-horse, and made a hurried step forward, uttering the word 'Sire!' in such a very pathetic tone that the instrument was immediately returned to him, and he was thus able to give his demonstration without again letting it out of his hands."[11]

To restore the Stanlein so that it appear brand new would be to deny its history, and this has been the operational dynamic from the start. It's not unlike the problem posed by restoration of a famed work of visual art; Michelangelo's Sistine Ceiling—to take just one example—aroused disapproval when cleaned. A principal measure of any such instrument's value, indeed, is how much original varnish remains intact; there's a quasi-pietistic faith in the properties of Stradivari's "secret" formula as an ingredient of sound. Greenhouse remembers the excitement with which Fernando Sacconi informed him

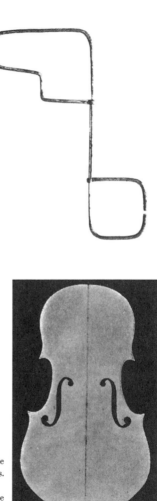

(*above*) Stradivari's calipers for the adjustment of thickness.

(*right*) Design by Stradivari for the outline and "*f*" holes of a small violin.

—on first encounter with the instrument—"There's enough varnish on this cello, original varnish, to have made three or four violins!"

So where Morel replaces the wood he imitates antiquity, replicating the grain of the spruce by brush-stroke (having copied the "original" on tracing paper and transferring every capillary to the patch), then adding microscopic black spots as though the recent surface had darkened over time. He has tried to match the colors of the top and back, since the latter is almost unsullied and the former much retouched. To my eye—admittedly an amateur's—the finished product eradicates distinction and evades detection; only when he holds the wood to the light and a par-ticular refractive angle, only when he points to it — "Here, Here!"—can I see where the "original" ends and its "imitation" begins.

$\int$

THE QUESTION OF VALUE IS A COMPLICATED ONE; IT too is subject to change. These instruments are rare enough to have no benchmark or average price, and this is more true of "that incomparable form of violoncello" — since there are so few of them — than the violin. When an important Van Gogh or Cezanne fetches tens of millions of dollars at auction, it's hard to escape the suspicion that a fine "Strad" remains undervalued. The 1727 Kreutzer Stradivarius (once owned by Rodolphe Kreutzer, for whom Beethoven wrote his violin sonata) was sold at auction in London for one-and-a-half million dollars in 1998; much more expensive purchases are prearranged and private. Experts agree or disagree; prices fluctuate from year to year and instrument to instrument — two, four, six million are being bruited now as sums — but the graph's curve points constantly up . . .

Consider this trajectory of purchase recorded by the Hills. "A violoncello dated 1730, the property of the Hon. Mr. Greaves, was offered for sale by auction at Messrs. Phillips'. It was brought in, and subsequently sold in 1866 to W.E. Hill, who resold it for £230 to Mr. Frederick Pawle. Purchased back in 1877 for £380, and resold to Mr. Edward Hennell in 1878 for £500. Again repurchased in 1880 for £475 and sold a few months later to Mr. C.G. Meier for £525. The instrument now migrated to Paris, and was there bought in 1882 from MM. Gand & Bernardel *frères* for £600 by Mr. David Johnson, and brought back to England, to be once again purchased by our firm in 1885 for £650."[12]

Although these amounts now seem laughably small, it's important to note the regularity with which the instrument was purchased; only once did it register a small decline—of twenty-five pounds—and in the course of nineteen years its value nearly trebled. That exponential pattern of increase remains the case today. Stradivari produced only two known guitars and twelve violas, a few dozen celli but hundreds of violins, and value is of course proportionate to scarcity. While the law of supply and demand still obtains, the price will continue to grow.

A skeptic might well raise an eyebrow as to how many "genuine" instruments keep being discovered in attics, or brought out of private collections; the number of certified Strads has almost doubled in the century since the Hill brothers (and thereafter Ernest Doring) compiled their lists. But even at its outer extent the

total is a small one, and the number still in "circula-
tion" (not owned by a collection or museum or bank)
decreases all the time.

$\int$

IN 1999 I "VISITED" THE CELLO AT REGULAR SPACED
intervals — in January, March, May, June, August,
October and November. In January and October
Greenhouse came along. It was rather like attending on
a much-loved patient in a nursing home or, more pre-
cisely, a hospital; the "Paganini Strad" lay broken —
shattered, albeit on purpose — and then in surgery and
traction and reconstruction until little by little she
healed. On first view — broken down into component
parts and contained in a stall in Morel's locked vault — the
cello appeared as forlorn as it must have to Merighi in
1822. In the streets of Milan it had lain on a barrow; in the
streets of Manhattan it stood in a bin, but only the trained

witness would think it a thing of great value or envision the instrument whole.

In addition to work on the varnish, the luthier had three principal tasks. The first was a patch near the top sound-post, which had been repaired before and unsuccessfully. The glue kept bleeding through miniscule cracks in the wood, and Morel had to remove and replace what had been ill done — most probably in the mid-nineteenth century. The second and more complicated project was repair work on the ribs, which had been both wormholed and previously buttressed — sometimes to the thickness of 2.5 millimeters where Stradivari himself had carved to the thickness of 1.5. Morel had to remove all the old glue and backing, then repair the damaged wood and steam the ribs again into their proper contours.

On May 13, 1999, for example, Morel takes a rib from its clamp. The wood has been in the clamp for five days, protected by padding and stretched to its original contour and its proper shape. There had been a doubling (a previous repair, with a second piece of wood glued on the inside), which the luthier removes. The original width of the maple was 1.5 millimeters, and three-tenths of a millimeter of intact maple remains. Morel takes a new piece of unblemished wood and shapes it to the Stanlein rib, following the contour of the original exactly and attaching the two with glue. Inside an airtight mold he lets the glue dry for two weeks. Then, removing it again, he reduces the width of the newly buttressed rib from 1.7 to 1.5 millimeters — thinning it down with a very sharp scraper to the desired thickness; smilingly he tells me, "You have to give it time."

Much the same procedure holds true for the spruce top, which had bellied up and flattened out under the stress of the sound-post and strings; this warp from "true" contour might seem infinitesimal, but it was redressed. For this purpose the luthier constructed a plaster cast in order to determine where there were, as he puts it, "bumps." The "Stanlein" top — delicately moistened in order to prove more malleable — was placed in a fiberglass mold. All during the summer of 1999 it lay encased in protective bindings — beneath a sheet of brown paper so the wood itself would not be touched, and then a sheet of wax paper, and then a sack of hot sand.

To return to the analogy of hospital and patient, by March of 2000 the cello's "bandages" had been removed and by April full-fledged "rehabilitation" began. The ribs were attached to the back. Several such "operations" had been concurrent if not simultaneous; work on the dissevered neck, for instance, was proceeding while the blocks (six buttressing slabs of wood to provide internal stability—one inside each of the corners, the bottom and top) were being shaped. In one case "I was able to remove the ribs from the block, because this block is original and I have to save it. See, this block is not original; Stradivari never used this; this is what I call a forest willow; when he used that one the willow was slightly reddish because of the aging, the oxidation, so I saved the original block. In this case I keep the original."

Each of the patches to the edge, each of the cracks and wormholes had to be varnished repeatedly (three coats at a minimum, more often more) and left to dry and made to merge with the "original" tint. At length the linings of the edge and the linen strips went in. "See those linings, they are very good; these are original. These"— Morel points to a separate half-inch strip of linen—"are not, but the guy did a fantastic job; still this I won't keep because I cannot remove it. Well, again, if they were original I would take one day to remove it, but if they're not

The Stanlein's scroll and the neck-block on which it fits.

original it doesn't pay; those from Stradivari's hand I go out of my way to save."

At the same time Morel was refashioning the neck. The block into which the neck fits was a combination of three or four previous repairs, and where the neck joins the scroll someone had shaved a segment off the pegbox; this was a delicate job indeed, since the "original" wood at this junction had been worn paper-thin. It had not cracked but was at risk; "I could have raised it with a bottom piece like it used to be at the turn of the century; instead I put a piece coming through from the inside out. If I'd fitted a patch it would have taken two hours; to do this is took me two days."

The neck itself had been replaced since Stradivari's time, and therefore, though exact, the act of substitution need not have been exacting. The fingerboard glued to the neck is fashioned out of ebony; the wood of the neck is maple and — rubbed with oil rather than varnished — should be contrasted to the color of the instrument as such. In his country property Morel keeps a barn full of wood, and with barely concealed excitement he shows me a segment of old maple purchased in France some thirty years before.

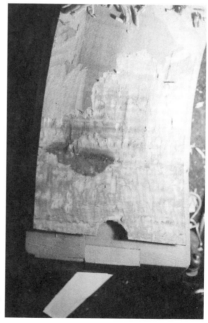

Cracked ribs and the ribs being fitted into molds; discussed on pages 77-78.

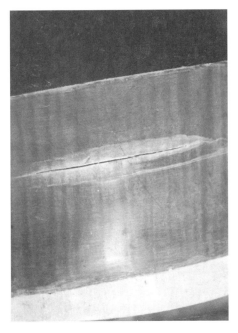

"Last weekend in the country I looked for pieces that I might use and I found—discovered again, in my attic—a piece of wood from Vuillaume. It was cut quite thick and came from the stock of my grandfather's shop; my grandfather, at the turn of the century, was dealing in wood for all the violin makers of France. This piece is definitely from Vuillaume, because my grandfather stamped *his* wood with the initials PM; this was cut with a circular saw—you can see it on the grain, the *maille*—because they used hydraulic power and electricity had not yet been invented."

What we look at, therefore—sent south from Paris to Marseilles, then shipped to New York and stored there in an upstate barn until used by Morel—is a piece of maple trimmed to shape and conjoined to an instrument built in Cremona. Now this reconstructed neck brings the wheel full circle; in the mid-1800's Paganini sold the instrument to Jean-Baptiste Vuillaume, and at the turn of the millennium a French luthier restores it with wood from Vuillaume's private stock.

$$\int$$

THE PROJECT HAD BEEN ESTIMATED TO TAKE SIX months, but by that date (March of 1999) it was clear that all hope of completion by summer would be wishful thinking, by summer the autumn, by autumn the start of the new year. As the months wore on, Morel began to allocate his Saturdays and Sundays to the project; no telephone rang in the closed weekend office, no customers appeared. When employed by Wurlitzer or Jacques Français the luthier could ignore matters of administration and a balance sheet; now as his own proprietor he had to pay attention. Where once the work could be uninterrupted, there now were the issues of getting and spending, and his profit margin as a dealer is far larger than as a restorer. In the former instance the sums could reach hundreds of thousands of dollars, in the latter tens, so his concentration was divided and his energy reduced.

"It may surprise you," he says, "but when I wake up at night I ask myself what I'm going to do, and then I make my plan. When I was young I'd make my plan, I'd tell myself I'm going to do this, this, *this*, and no matter how long it would take I would finish it; today if I do two-thirds of what I've planned I'm very pleased with myself, because my head is getting ahead of my physique. When I come home at the end of the day my eyes tear; I try to watch a little bit of the news and I can't even do that because it's very tiring. When you work all day with a magnifying glass it's very very tiring, because the focus shifts. For instance when I paint these grains here, I work very close, sometimes so close that I cut the end of my brush because it touches my magnifying glass, but my hands are still steady, thank God. I keep saying if my eyes were as good as my hands I would still work like when I was thirty. But in this class of restoration it's the last one I can do . . . "

At eighty-four, Greenhouse had grown sleepless also. "During many hours awake in the night," he says, "and even in my dreams I've thought about the instrument; when I first saw it in its dismantled form—lying on the bench in pieces—I stroked the ribs, almost as though it was a body, a living thing. I've traveled the world with that instrument; it's been my companion for forty years. It was my career, my *friend*.

"Of course I did have moments when I thought that, in this last period of my life, I could simply have had the pleasure of playing the instrument, of keeping it at hand. I have to fight to keep away from the telephone;

my instinct is to call René every day and say, hey, did you do anything, has anything happened today? But each time I remind myself that things should be done to the instrument, they should have been done before my time, and I thought I owed a debt to the cello. I thought that it had done its service for me, I owed a service to it."

$$\int$$

IN FAIRY TALES ALL THINGS MAY BE RESTORED. THAT which disappeared is found and that which was hidden revealed. The crone transforms herself to princess when kissed by a sufficient prince; the old grow young and fair and unblemished and supple once more. To imagine the Countess of Stanlein first played is to people the candlelit hall with an audience: stiff-backed gentlemen bewigged and bright-eyed ladies whispering behind their fluttered fans. The shade of Niccolò Paganini hovers nearby somewhere also—elongated,

passionate, and bent above the bow. Or earlier—
Merighi, and those who came to visit the maker himself
in Cremona—the ones who came to purchase or to
lodge an order or perhaps apprentice to the trade. Who
knows what Greenhouse dreamed that day he shut his
eyes and saw himself a youth once more, agile, in the
Pyrenees and learning from Casals?

In such a dream a cello floats upon the perfumed air.
Ethereal, corporeal, it is the shape and very contour of
encapsulated sound. Its archings are perfectly rounded
and smooth; its varnish gleams; the purfling lends a
definition and a darkness to the edge. From volute
scroll to seamless rib the pattern of the wood itself is
intrinsicate with melody, suggestive of a promised plen-
itude: yet resonant, yet mute.

On Tuesday, May 23, 2000, Greenhouse travels once
more to New York. Morel has spent the weekend ready-
ing the cello for delivery—returning the strings he
removed in 1998, making adjustments to the sound-post
and to his newly cut bridge. He has prepared for this
transfer carefully, stage-managing it to the last detail:
an impresario. It is eleven o'clock. Greenhouse, arriving,
palpably nervous, says "I have dreamed of this

René Morel in his workshop, the cello complete.

moment, I can't wait to see it, first I want to see it and then hold it and then touch the bow to the strings. But before that I have to warm up."

Morel conducts him to a secondary office and produces a Stradivarius that was built with a flat back. "It's one of two Stradivari built where he tried out a flat back," he says. "But this one is cut down, its back is not

89

original. You can buy it if you wish . . . " The sound of the
cello is muted and nasal, but Greenhouse plays it nevertheless, tentative at first and elsewhere-focused; he is
wondering, he tells me, if his own Strad's tone will have
changed. "My fingers feel like sausages," he says. After
some time Morel reappears. "Are we ready, Maestro?"

In the large room at the atelier's rear there are
signed photographs of Pablo Casals and Mischa Elman
and Isaac Stern and photographs of Albert Einstein
and Fritz Kreisler; cello-cases range like sentries at
attention down the wall. Morel has placed a solid chair
for the performer to sit on and, at the room's far end—
some twenty feet distant, his back to the window—a
second chair where he himself will listen in order to
gauge projection. "All I did," he tells me, smiling, "was
change the strings. It has taken me two years because I
am very slow."

We laugh. Greenhouse is wearing glasses. Like a
father with a newborn child or husband with a long-lost
bride, he receives the cello, embracing it, cradling it
tenderly. He examines the ribs, the front, the back, then
turns the instrument upside down and reverses it again.
He traces the edging, the purfling, the scroll. "Oh,

René," he breathes. "It's beautiful. Bravo!" At length he starts to play. He tries the open strings, tries fingerings, tries scales and then searches for "wolf" notes—the place where the cello's vibrations might clash and make the sound, wobbling, go flat. Instead in the echoing space of this room the sound is pure, powerful, bright. "The *voice*," says the musician, "it's just what I remember—what I've been hearing in my head. Exactly how she sang before . . . "

In a week or a month or a year, perhaps, Morel will make adjustments—but not now, not today. "There's nothing to adjust," the men agree.

Then there is lunch. This is a celebration, and we walk to a French restaurant in the neighborhood. Emmanuel Gradoux-Matt joins the party, and the four of us order champagne. "*An die Musik*" I offer, and Morel and Gradoux-Matt, clicking glasses, say, "*Santé*," and Greenhouse says "Tchin-Tchin." Close attention is paid to the menu and then to the prospect of food.

"But the red wine with the *entrée*," cautions Morel. "They serve it too cold here. We should have the waiter bring it already. In this matter they are not quite correct. It has to be *chambrée*."

(*above*) Substitute bridges and strings; the traveling tools of the trade.

(*right*) Morel adjusting the sound-post and bridge in the hotel, on the last day.

(*opposite*) "The Countess of Stanlein," René Morel and Bernard Greenhouse in the hotel room in Towson, Maryland.

"Are you booked on the five o'clock flight? The six o'clock?" I ask my father-in-law. "What do you plan to do now?"

"I'm going to put my cello in its case and take a taxi to the airport and buy it a ticket and carry it home." Greenhouse raises his glass. "And we will never ever be separated again."

$$\int$$

THE WORLD CELLO CONGRESS DESERVES ITS APPEL-lation; players come from all over the world. Those who have been chosen, via audition, to be taught in "Master Classes" include citizens of Brazil, Bulgaria, China, Croatia, France, Germany, Ireland and Poland, as well as the USA. The recent rise in the instrument's popularity has given equivalent rise to the number of practitioners; next year a gathering of a "thousand cellists" is scheduled for Japan. To see two hundred cellists on the stage in Baltimore— as was the case in the final concert of the Congress on Saturday, June 3—is to listen to sound unimagined by Boccherini or Bach.

The first group to perform comes from Korea (the "Beehouse Cello Ensemble," named in honor of Bernard Greenhouse and wearing traditional Korean garb), the next from the Toho Conservatory in Tokyo. Then, after intermission, two hundred members of the "Massed Cello Ensemble" crowd the stage of Meyerhoff Symphony Hall. Half as many again have been turned away in rehearsal, since the stage cannot accommodate everyone, but the sense of celebration is palpable: serious play. There are world-class performers and avid amateurs together, the elderly and youthful bowing in unison. They perform specially commissioned pieces and transcriptions from Villa-Lobos and Ralph Vaughan Williams and John Phillips Sousa and even the theme from "Mission Impossible"; the audience applauds.

Then Greenhouse is announced and two-hundred cellists stamp their feet — a drum-roll of appreciation for the Congress's "Artistic Advisor." This will be his first appearance in the full space of a concert hall, the first time the cello "sounds out." All week he has been wor-

rying, practicing, making adjustments. So has René
Morel. At the conference on Thursday morning Morel
gave a speech, discussing the technique of instrument
making and repair, its challenges, its history. "I believe a
lecture should be like a woman's skirt," he says. "Long
enough to cover the subject, short enough to keep it
interesting." He discourses on the physics of sound, the
general problems of restoration and "Cello Making for
Today's Virtuoso."

"There's nobody like him," says Timothy Eddy of the
Orion Quartet. "He truly understands the relationship
between all aspects of an instrument's physical condition
and set-up, its sound quality and responsiveness."

"He camouflaged his work so beautifully," agrees Paul
Katz of the Cleveland Quartet. Both have had their instruments—a Matteo Goffriller and Andrea Guarneri respec-
tively—restored in Morel's atelier; both praise his expertise.

But each day in the hotel suite Greenhouse and Morel
have been "fiddling" with the "Stanlein's" sound-post,
shifting its position so as to apply greater or less pressure
to the top. Since he wants a set-up with which he is
familiar, Greenhouse shifts bridges also, first trying the
original Sacconi bridge, then the one Martin Cornellisen

cut for his own copy of the instrument. "It doesn't fit," protests the luthier. "You can put a dime under its feet. It's a good bridge, I'm not saying anything against the bridge —but not for this cello," he says.

Greenhouse is unconvinced. "The strings sit too high with the one that you cut for me. You listen to it in this room, your ears are excellent, of course, I trust them absolutely, but I'm the one who plays. And it's too hard with this bridge."

"But that will change," Morel repeats. "The top has been lying alone for a year and a half; it will need to be adjusted. A month from now, *Maître*, you bring it back to the shop. And then"—he spreads his hands—"we will see what we hear."

What they see and hear in the concert hall is the refurbished instrument, its sound resplendent now. Greenhouse plays the solo in "Song of the Birds"—a Catalan folk-song transcribed for the cello by Pablo Casals. "'I have performed it,'" the musician says his teacher told him, "'hundreds, hundreds of times.'" It's a simple melody, an evocation of bird-calls and flight, an easy line to play and difficult to master. This is mastery. Greenhouse has his eyes half-shut, his old head bending heavily, his feet and hands and body engaged, his cello in his arms. Behind him rank on rank of cellists listen and respond. "There were tears in our eyes," says Lluís Claret, himself a Catalan. "There were many of us crying."

The audience erupts. Greenhouse rises, bows, accepts flowers. "He has moved beyond music," the man to my left, standing, says.

NOTES

1   Hill, W. Henry, Hill, Arthur F., & Hill, Alfred E., *Antonio Stradivari, His Life & Work, (1644-1737)*, Dover Publications, Inc., New York, *1963*, (unabridged republication of original volume, W. E. Hill & Sons, 1902), p. 20.

2   This description derives from: Cowling, Elizabeth, *The Cello*, Charles Scribner's Sons, New York, 1975, pps. 17–19.

3   Doring, Ernest, *How Many Strads? Our Heritage from the Master; A Tribute to the Memory of a Great Genius, compiled in the year marking the Tercentenary of his birth; being a Tabulation of Works Believed to Survive Produced in Cremona by Antonio Stradivari, Between 1666 and 1737, including relavant data and mention of his two sons Francesco and Omobono*, William Lewis & Son, Chicago, 1945, p. 19.

NOTES

4 Piatigorsky, Gregor, *Cellist*, Doubleday & Co., New York, 1965, pps. 259–60.

5 Curtin, Joseph, email communication to author, 5/15/00.

6 Cowling, Elizabeth, op. cit., p. 52.

7 Hill, op. cit., p. 132.

8 Ibid, pps. 124–129.

9 Curtin, Joseph, "Innovation in Violinmaking," Joseph Curtin Studios, 205 N. Main St., Ann Arbor, MI

10 Hill, op. cit., pps. 1 32-33.

11 Doring, op. cit., pps. 161-62.

12 Hill, op. cit, p. 273.

INDEX

INDEX

CREDITS

This book is an expanded version of an article that first appeared as a folio in *Harper's* magazine, January, 2001.

IMAGES

All photographs are by Nicholas Delbanco, unless otherwise noted.

Frontispiece courtesy Stewart Pollens for *Strad* magazine

p. 8   Bernard Greenhouse Collection

p. 16   from *Antonio Stradivari: His Life and Work*, W. Henry Hill, Arthur F. Hill & Alfred E. Hill.

p. 17   from *Antonio Stradivari: His Life and Work*, W. Henry Hill, Arthur F. Hill & Alfred E. Hill.

p. 18   Bernard Greenhouse Collection

p. 22   Bernard Greenhouse Collection

p. 23   Bernard Greenhouse Collection

p. 29   Courtesy KLM Royal Dutch Airlines Photo

p. 31   Bernard Greenhouse Collection

p. 52   Bernard Greenhouse Collection

p. 53   Courtesy Whitestone Photo

p. 66   Bernard Greenhouse Collection

p. 67   Bernard Greenhouse Collection

p. 72   from *Antonio Stradivari: His Life and Work*, W. Henry Hill, Arthur F. Hill & Alfred E. Hill.